Book Titles
by Authors

Book Titles by Authors

Best with custard by
Stu Dapples

Tony Wooliston

Library of Congress Control Number:		2018906432
ISBN:	Hardcover	978-1-5434-9066-4
	Softcover	978-1-5434-9065-7
	eBook	978-1-5434-9064-0

Print information available on the last page.

Rev. date: 05/31/2018

To order additional copies of this book, contact:
Xlibris
800-056-3182
www.Xlibrispublishing.co.uk
Orders@Xlibrispublishing.co.uk
774216

PROLOGUE

When putting together a piece of literature of this magnitude, there is just one final thing that I want to say that is not already said, and none-the-less for that, not to put too finer point on it, and taking everything into account, allowing for all eventualities, we should never forget, that far be it for me to say that in the vast majority of instances this has been the case, and as we all know, and lets not sweep this under the carpet, because it has often been said eventually and not too far off the day will dawn when this will manifest itself and believe me there will be some red faces then with egg all over them. But as we have seen many times before, and it is well worth repeating this that all my friends will bear me out on this and we're not ashamed to say that I am not alone here and neither should I be.

Personally speaking in the final analyses at the end of the day, between You and me and leaving all else aside, weighing everything up by and large and in the heat of the moment when all else is said and done (Else won't be coming by the way) – as far as I am concerned let's get it out in the open and to tell you the honest truth I'll be glad to see the back of it.

BOOK SUMMARY

This book has no plot, no start and no finish. It is a collection over many years of an imaginary book written by an imaginary author ... 'The hunchback' by Stan Upstrate. If you don't get it try again or get Percy Vere to help you.

Guilty as charged by
Y Deedoit

The Collector

These titles have been collected by Tony Wooliston, who is retired and lives in Oxfordshire.

With grateful thanks to Mike for his wonderful pictures ...
... and to Gary for his patience with a forgetful old man.

2

The bald facts	by	Al Apeesha
Drunk Every Night	by	Al K Hollick
Beware of the Dog	by	Al Sayshun
Follow The Yellow Brick Road	by	Alison Wonderland

Course of treatment by
Anna Bollick-Steroids

Don't fight with her	by	Ally Kat
He's in love with her	by	Ann Admirer
Oh ... by the way	by	Anna Nutherthing
A lovely day for a wedding	by	Annabel Wozringing

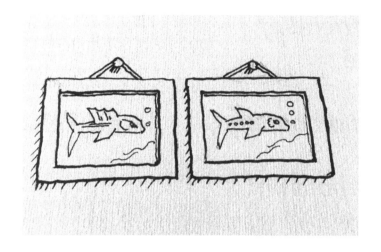

Not quite the same by
Arty Fishull

No friend of mine   by   Arch Enemy

Island hopping   by   Archie Pelago

Just hold on there   by   Arfur Minute

From the top   by   Ariel View

The self-made man by
Claude Iswayup

The grand mansion	by	Austin Tayshus
Cashflow problems	by	Baxter Thewall
Touch your toes	by	Ben Dover
The drunk monk	by	Benny Dictine

Watch the sugar by
Di Abetic

Can he run Faster ?	by	Betty Can't
Can't hit a barn door	by	Betty Misses
Settle your account Sir ?	by	Bill Pending
Let us pray	by	Neil Downe

Cold outside by
Don McCoat

Explosive on Sunday	by	Cannon Fodder
She's lovely	by	Carrie Smattic
Lend us your wheels	by	Carter Riding
Better go now	by	Casey Comesback

Got rid of the body by
Doug Deep

The spin Doctor	by	Catherine Wheel
Fair play to 'em	by	Cher N'Cheralike
Hold on a second	by	Chester Minnit
Off to A&E	by	Chez Paynes

Up at dawn by
Earl E. Riser

Beautiful under water	by	Coral Reef
Be sure it's well cooked	by	Crispin Damiddle
How long will it take?	by	Daisy Sedd
Enjoy retirement	by	Dec Creppid

Your table is ready by
Ed Waiter

Irish skin specialist	By	Dermot Ology
Best biscuit recipes	by	Di Gestive
She'll open up	by	Dora Jarr
We tried everything	by	Drew A'blank

Away with the fairies by
Edna Cloud

Let some light in by Drew Curtainsback

Central office by Ed Quarters

How to get in by Eileen Back

When the bomb went off by Ella Vabang

What's the price? by
Emma Chisset

Where to see the game	by	Doug Out
He's only a little 'un	by	Eardley Biggenuff
You'd better do it	by	Elsie Will
Can't believe a word he says	by	Ely Salott

No swearing by
Polly Curses

A changed man   by   Esau Thelight

In big trouble   by   Evan Elpus

Get there in the end   by   Eve Entually

The priest has gone   by   Father Away

This is not my suit ! by
Fitz Imbetta

Michael row the boat	by	Eve Hoe
Moor up over there	by	Eve Too
The 3 nuns	by	Faith Hop'ncharity
True believer	by	Faith Ingod

The channel hopper by
Francis Close

The loose bolt by Finn Gertite

Can't see eye to eye by Greeta Differ

She's seen the light by Dawn Onyer

Invite everybody by Hall Ansundry

When's the next bus? by
Harper Six

Smoker's cough	by	Flem Boyant
The honest politician	by	Frank N Open
Keep your voice down	by	Freddy Mitehear
The war is over	by	Freeda Prisoners

The Bald German by
Herr Missing

Bad weather	by	Gail Force-Winds
It was a dull day	by	Grace Kize
Egyption wallpaper	by	Ira Gliffix
It's dark in here	by	Isaach Customising

The flat camel by
Hump Free

Nice paper   by   Hannah Glipta

Who told you?   by   Hedda Phone-Call

You can see forever   by   Honor Clearday

Fingers crossed   by   Hope Allswell

Wait for me by
Isaac Cummin

Warm as toast	by	Ida Down
Blunder on in	by	Inigo Edfust
Lucky to survive	by	Innes Condition
There are no buses	by	Ira Carr

Not tonight Josephine by
Ivan Edache

On top of the mountain	by	Isiah Thanyou
Over the whole house	by	Ivy Kreeps
The taxi's waiting	by	Izzy Cummin
Would you care to join me?	by	Jean Antonic

Relax in the tub by
Jack Oozey

The source of the power	by	Jen Erator
Emergency petrol	by	Jerry Can
Under starter's orders	by	Jocelyn Forraplace
Are you serious?	by	Joe King

The thumbless Judge by
Justice Fingers

Butcher's best	by	Joyce Cutlets
Salt It away	by	Kay Manislands
It's cold outside	by	Ken Eyecummin
How many are there?	by	Ken Eyehaveone

Facing disaster by
Kat Astrophy

Can I borrow your couch?	by	Kip Down
My night in A&E	by	Lance Maboil
I'm innocent	by	Laura Byding
She's on the doorstep	by	Letta Inn

Potting for beginners by
Lief Mold

She liked the girls   by   Lez Behan

On parade   by   Linus Hupp

The human cannonball   by   Lotta Bottle

British Rail tea   by   Luke Warm

They took it all by
Kit Chensink

Falsify attendance	by	Marcus Present
Nice paint job	by	Matt Finnish
Anything can happen	by	May Bee
The story of club-books	by	Mel Order-catalogue

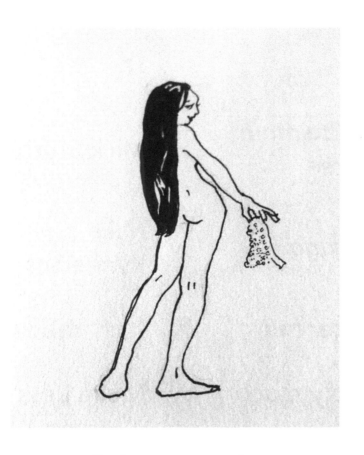

Bedroom capers by
Lacey Knickers

Add to main course	by	Mick Sturbs
Chicago	by	Mike Kyndertown
Better hurry	by	Miss Yabuss
Pretty much	by	Moira Less

Once bitten by
Nesta Vipers

The spoilt child	by	Molly Cuddle
Is that what happened?	by	Mustaffa Gotten
Before I pass sentence	by	N E Previous
Seek forgiveness	by	Neil Andpray

Cold parts by
Nick Erless

It's all been for nothing	by	Noah Vale
Baby's revenge	by	Nora Nippleov
The fuller figure	by	Norma Snockers
Noisy dog (The musical)	by	Offenbach

They're at the gates by
Norman Conquest

He's only got one speed   by   Onslo Motion

Die In debt   by   Owen Munny

The half blind pirate   by   Pat Choverwunni

There's a hole in my sock   by   Fred Bear

The neighbour from Birmingham by
Olive Nextdoor

Long queue at A&E	by	Patience Please
Irish double-glazing	by	Patty O' Door
Don't give up	by	Pearce E Veer
The pirate's wife	by	Pegg Legg

I couldn't put it down by
Paige Turner

A guide to pound shops	by	Penny Pinching
I'm being bullied	by	Percy Kution
The money is all gone	by	Percy Sempty
Dig for cheaper fuel	by	Pete Bogg

Man's best friend by
Pat Thedog

The money's nearly gone	by	Peter Ringout
Better than diesel	by	Petra Lenjin
He gave it all away	by	Phil Anthropic
Chinese tummy bugs	by	Phil Ling Funny

Scared to death by
Petra Fied

He is not bothered by it by Phil O'Soffical

Load of rubbish by Phillipa Dustbin

Have you got an invitation? by Phyllis Cumming

Brighton's burning by Piers Onfire

Get stuck in lad by
Phil Maboots

Goes well with an Indian	by	Pitta bread
Cover all the cracks	by	Polly Filla
Who owns Monaco ?	by	Prince Ipality
Won the lottery	by	Prince Le Sum

He won again by
Vic Toreus

Watchword caution   by   Pru Denshal

My life on the Great Western   by   Ray Wailtrax

She travelled a lot   by   Rhoda Bike

We're in the big league   by   Rich N'famuss

Concreting made easy by
Will Barrow

Tug of war secrets	by	Paul Together
The tap's in the street	by	Walter Main
The uprising	by	Jacob Behan
Who's to blame?	by	Sue Ford-damages

Dangerous jobs in the kitchen by
Piers Thelid

On The Rebound	by Rick O'Shay
Hail a cab in Hong Kong	by Rick Shaw
A big lad	by Rio Grande
He stole from pensioners	by Robin Bastard

Warm in winter by
Walter Wallcarpet

Like a lion by Rory Sedd

Cripples your knees by Ruth Tyler

We're on our way by Sally Forth

Mouth-watering stuff by Sally Vate

He's in the percussion section by
Tam Boreen

The Spanish lottery	by	Senor Munnyin
The Spanish buffet lunch	by	Senorita Nutherpie
Only yourself to blame	by	Sevvy Wright
Good ole girl	by	Sheila Blige

What's it all mean? by
Sym Bollical

That can't be true	by	Shirley Knott
Happy go lucky	by	Sonny Disposition
The hunchback	by	Stan Upstrate
Needs a hearing aid	by	Stephanie Karneer

Listen up Moses! by
Seth Thelord

Old as the hills	by	Terry Dectil
Never puts his hand in his pocket	by	Titus Adrum
My day will come	by	Wendy Boat-Kumsin
The yobbo	by	Will Fulldamage

A bigger house by
Sammy Detached

How I gave up	by	Will Power
Will he do that?	by	Willy Eckerslike
He eats like a pig	by	Wolf Sisfood
The dentist	by	Y Dopen

Wet floors by
Rufus Leakin

Perfect with a cuppa	by	Rich Tee
Another year older	by	Annie Versary
She will put a damper on it	by	April Showers
'E don't look well	by	Art Attack

The outboard's broken by
Rowan Back

It'll do yer good	by	Benny Fishil
Late already	by	Buster Catch
Blossoms in spring	by	Chris Anthemum
Is there anybody there ?	by	Clair Voyant

Healthy girls by
Rosie Cheeks

Dropped right in it	by	Dee Pend
The substitute	by	Innes Place
All squashed in	by	Tina Sardines
Hold the bus	by	Gerry Atrics

You're not invited by
M. Bargo

Acknowledgements

The author is indebted to the following servicemen for their contribution to the military section of this book …

- General Factotum
- Colonel Bogey
- Major Cockup
- Corporal Punishment, and
- Private Parts …

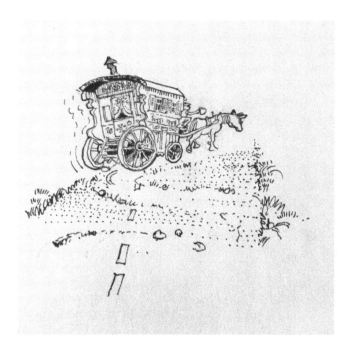

Caravanning for beginners by
Wanda Rabout